POEMS FOR THE BROKEN HEARTED

NIGEL EDWARDS

Also By Nigel Edwards...

Untamed Series...

Vol 1 - The Taming of Cambridge

Vol 2 - An Untamed Mind

Featured in...

Platonic - Eternal Love

(Poetry Anthology)

For mum and dad

ALWAYS LOVE YOU

I don't know what is inside my head,
Trying to remember what she said.
Don't know if she wanted to go bed,
Will it be the same until I'm dead?

Most of them just don't care,
It's not our time, won't share.
Never been so happy as when she was there.

Won't ever have another chance,
Doesn't matter what I want to ask.

Won't ever be happy in my home,
Why won't you even call on the phone?
Can't help but think are you alone?

Maybe I need some more to drink.
Will it be the same today,
Tomorrow,
And next week.

It's like you can't even remember my name.
I will always love you,
I know you don't feel the same.

AGAIN

Will I ever see you again?
I don't know what to say.
Will this be our last day?

When I walk down the street,
and people ask who will you meet?
I always think of you,
Told you I loved you,
You know this to be true.

I can't change the way I feel,
Do you not feel safe?
Do you think I will steal?

Is there anything I can do?
Please say you love me too.

APART

I had the most wonderful dream,
We were at the circus eating ice cream.
Holding hands and having fun,
You knew that you were my one.

But when I woke up,
I remembered we broke up,
And felt so sad,
For the life we could have had.

Feel like I'm no-one and I don't belong,
my love has gone.
Not looking forward to this new day,
Is there nothing I can do to make you stay?

I remembering looking into your eyes,
I won't tell you a single lie.
Without you I can't heal my heart,
I never wanted us to be apart.

BELIEVE

I don't know how to be happy,
I don't know me.
No-one knows me.
I never feel free.
Don't want to be me.

I'll try and try,
Do you want me to cry?
And say that I lie?
I will still try.

Won't give up, need love.
Can I be want you need?
Will you laugh when I bleed?
What will I achieve?
Will you believe?

BELONG

Have I lost you?
You said you only love me a little bit.

Echos in my head,
Even when I'm sleeping in bed.
I can remember what you said.

You know how I feel,
You know it's real.

I miss you, whenever your not there,
You know that I care.

Will it only exist in a memory?
I know I have done wrong, but with you I belong.

I CAN REMEMBER

I can remember the first time I saw you,
I can remember the words you said.
Our love was so strong,
I know I did wrong.

I won't ever be the same,
I want to see you again.
It has been so much time,
Since you were mine.

I don't know how to explain how I feel,
But my heart just won't heal.
I've been having weird dreams,
Just part of a machine.

I'm there but can't be seen,
You asked where have I been?
Can you ever forgive?
I will love you as long as I live.

CAN'T GO ON

I can't continue this way,
Tomorrow always the same as today.
Maybe I knew this from the start,
Life with you was never a walk in the park.

When I close my eyes,
I remember all the lies.
I know what you are,
You can't disguise.

I don't want to be unkind,
But you will be left behind.
You have got nowhere to hide.

CANDLE LIGHT

Missing the one I love,
Is there a heaven above?
Will I ever a able to see her again?
How can life ever be the same?

I'll go to sleep and wake up again,
It is always the same.
I'm broken and don't know how to repair,
Everyday I wish she was there.

Waiting for the moonlight,
Don't know what I'm doing tonight.
Want to hold you tight in the candle light.

I know I can go anywhere,
But you will not be there.

DO KNOW

I do know my own heart,
and have done from the start.
I Want to send you art.
Where can we go?
What can we do?
You know I love you.
The words I want to say.
Will you break my heart?
I will do it for love's sake.

YOU DON'T LOVE ME

The ship has already sailed,
I have bailed.

My hopes and dreams,
Have turned into screams.
Need to calm down,
Need to look around.

While I'm listening to the sound,
the people, walking around on the ground.
None of this seems to matter that much,
Unlike us, they're all so out of touch.

Though, then It all gets a little fuzzy,
Why it is you don't love me?
I know I've got to move on,
But the voice in my head screams out,
"Where have you gone?"

I don't want to live in a dream,
But living life without you feels so obscene.
It is now all I can see,
The truth that you don't love me.

But when I wake up,
I remember the brake up,
And feel so sad,
Missing the life we could have had.

DON'T STAY

Will it make you cry?
Trying to lie?
Tell me how you feel inside.
Do you try to bottle it up?

Is it not lost love?
Don't tell me this doesn't hurt,
What is it worth?

I will live my life without you,
Not caring what you do.
If you gave me a call,
I wouldn't answer at all.

It doesn't matter what you say.
I don't want you to stay.

I'll try and try,
Do you want me to cry?
And say that I lie?
I will still try.

DON'T UNDERSTAND

You accuse me of crimes I didn't commit,
and sit there and say come on, give me a hit.
That man is such a fool,
Nothing but a tool.

I can't understand the reason why,
That with him it's always a lie.
And then when I ask why,
All I get is a stupid sigh.

Not sure what to say,
This is not play.
When I wake up,
It's a new day.

What is it like?
When you don't know how to live your life?
A man with no kids or wife,
Like a plane taking a nose dive.

And like that plane,
I will crash into the ground.
I don't understand why,
What's the point of living a lie?

ALL I EVER WANTED

I can remember when we first met,
Feels like such a long time ago,
Don't want you to be someone I used to know.
I never wanted to go,
Why didn't I answer the phone?

This isn't a trick,
My heart feels sick.
But you gave me another chance,
You are more than I could ever ask.

We went out and had fun,
You will always be the only one.
I ruined it again,
Got only myself to blame.

Don't understand myself,
Is there a problem with my mental health?

They say I should move on,
That I've got to stay strong.
There is no point in anything I do,
none of them have a clue.

All I ever wanted to do is love you.

DREAMING

I can't remember if it was a dream.
Will this love be unseen?
Waiting for you to come home,
I can't stand my mind when I'm alone.

I roll over in bed,
Thinking about what you said.
You were so happy to see me,
I'd been waiting all day long.
And then you were gone.

As soon as I fall asleep,
In my mind I heard you speak.
It seemed so real, you know how I feel.

Then I open my eyes,
And I realise there is no point telling lies.

What can I do?
So much I want to undo.

DREAMS

I hear it in whispers,
I hear it in screams,
I hear the voice crying out,
Inside my dreams.

It's not all is as it seems,
Not everyone agrees.
Why should I care what they say?
I don't want any of them to stay.

They don't know my heart,
Treating me like I'm not even.
What have they seen?

Inside my soul,
I don't feel whole.
All scrambled up,
I need your love.

The most important thing in the world,
I feel so cold.
Need somewhere to belong,
With people who know where I'm from.

Wish I could see you again,
It's driving me insane.

WHISPER

Heard it in a whisper,
Heard it in a dream.
The girl I love was with me,
You are all I can see.

So many things come and go,
Confusing me,
Abusing my muse,
It's all a ruse that you choose.

Want it to be more clear,
You are the most important thing.
All the words people say,
Always seem the same.

Is there anything I can do,
That will be important to you?
Miss you so much it makes me sick,
Don't know what to think.

My life is in a mess,
And Ican't even give it a guess.
If only I could see you again,
All of my dreams have floated away.

EMPTY INSIDE

Going to try with all my heart,
But all I can do is say I want to see you.
They all treat me like I don't have a clue,
There has to be something I can do.

I don't want to give up,
I need your love.
Didn't we have fun?

We can stay in bed all day,
Or go out to play.
Don't want to live in a dream,
I screwed it up, don't deserve your love.

Got to get used to the idea,
You don't want me near.
Feel empty inside,
Want you to know never lied.

What is the point?
We will never be together,
And I don't feel clever.

You are the most important thing in the world to me,
Please don't say it will never be.

ENDING

I can't wait to see you again,
But don't know what you will say.
Feel this way everyday,
Thinking about what to say.
Always wishing you could stay.

Whenever you are not there,
I look forward to seeing you.

When you smile,
And say you want me to stay.
You make me feel,
This could be real.

I never want this to end,
Want to be more than just a friend.

EVERYDAY

Waiting in the bus station,
Got so much time, the rain keeps pouring down.
Everybody around can see my frown,
A girl tried to smile at me, but I'm feeling so down.
She had a look of disappointment in her eyes,
Could her smile reveal her lies?

Had enough, lost the one I love.
Trying to enjoy my day, the games I can play.
With people who want me to stay.

I don't want to tell them how I feel,
I want to pretend love isn't real.

Can fake it up, of course I remember your name,
Good to see you again.
My heart is in pain,
Everyday is the same.

EVERYTHING

When you put your hands on me,
I know eternal love is free.

When you whisper in my ear,
And you make yourself clear.

You make my heart light up the dark.
As soon as I see you, I can't hide how I feel.

I want to spend my life loving you,
In everything I do.
Do I mean anything?
You are everything.

FAR AWAY

Everyday is the same,
or at least it seem that way.
People are so lame,
What they say is always the same.

The pattern repeats,
It's enough to make me weep.
I wonder if they ever think,
Are they all sheep?

How did we put man on the moon?
Things aren't going to change any time soon.
Got to get up for another day,
The memories of her love, seems so far away.

I think about her everyday,
To hell with what people say.
I can't live with the thought of never seeing her again.
Don't want my heart to feel this much pain.

I'll get up for another day,
But I know it will be the same.

FEELING DOWN

Got to get back on my feet,
Sort my head out,
And take a walk down the street.
There is no-one I want to meet.

I could pretend,
But when they talk,
I just want it to end.

I fake it up a little bit,
But don't really want to do it.
Friends tell me I shouldn't be so down,
I should focus and turn my life around.

Don't want anyone around,
Going to stay down.

I walked past where you used to live,
Knowing you won't forgive.
I want to call but you will treat me like a fool.
Just hoping tomorrow will be a better day,
But it will be the same anyway.

GONE

I can't do this anymore,
I can't have fun.
Feel like I'm no-one,
It's my fault your gone.

Every time I hear your name,
Everything I do seems in vain.
It burns my soul,
Making me feel like I'm not whole.

Never meant to let you down,
They treat me like I'm a clown.
Every time I look hurt,
They asked if I've learned.

Then it's time to go to bed alone,
And I want to call you on the phone.
I would love to hear your voice,
But you will say I have no choice.

If only I could speak to you again,
This is driving me insane.
Got to find the strength to carry on,
But I know you are the only one.

GOODBYE KISS

When it's late at night,
I don't want to fight.

Confused by the reason why I try.
You will mock me if I cry, and say I'm to shy.

Still want to try, not going to give up,
You will always be the one I love.
We could live into old age,
And I know that won't change.

I won't listen to them,
Saying I should try again.
I'm sick of this,
You won't even give me a good bye kiss.

GOODBYE

Will you make a fool out of me?
Will you lie and make me cry?
Is it always my fault?
Give me another insult.
Was it never fun?

Trying my heart out,
No need to shout.
Why so angry,
Don't you even know me?

Need this to change,
you're my favourite person in the world,
Have been told.
Can say good bye, why do I try?

HAUNTING

Every time I think of you,
I don't know what to do.
I Can't change the past,
Ask the questions I want to ask.

Does it matter to you?
Can I have a clue?
Haunted by the memories,
Will I never be free?

What you did to me,
Can I never see?
Was it my fault?
Hide it in the occult.

HELL

My life is a living hell,
Like I have been cast under an evil spell.
There is no fun, and its boring,
It is a living horror story.

I think I caught your eye,
But I'm too shy.
They can all take the piss, are they having fun?
Calling me a bum.

Its a simple mentality,
Don't they get reality?
Find it hard to communicate,
Why do I get so much hate?

Then they want to call my girl a whore,
Even though we're not together anymore.
I will be happy when they are not there,
I know they don't care.

Love is stronger than hate,
It is something they should appreciate.
I Love you all the time,
And wish you were still mine.

HOME

I can remember last December,
When we were still together.
Not caring about the weather,
Weren't we so clever.
On that day, not made out of clay.
All I wanted to say, was I need you everyday.
I wouldn't have it any other way.
And when I'm on my own,
Will we live in the same home?

HOME ALONE

Don't want to go home alone, please come with me.
I know you are free, and will say it's nothing to do
with me.
Can't see, don't want you to be just a memory.
Can't undo what I did wrong, making me feel sick
inside.
My feelings I can't hide, they will take me for a ride.
Trying to think of something to say, something that will
make you stay.
Is there anything I can do to make you smile?
Will go that extra mile.
When you look at me with love in your eyes, my love for
you I can't disguise.
If only I could have one more try, my love for you is
no lie.

FEELS LIKE HOME

I don't know how to be happy,
Home

All the people that I meet,
And the people on the street.
I will listen to every word,
What have I learned?
When they want attention,
There is always a lesson.
If you can't be smart then be mature,
With most of them I'm not sure.
What is it all for?
When I feel like I can't take any more.
Need to know where I belong,
You know where I'm from.
I know with you it feels like home.

HOPE YOU UNDERSTAND

You keep confusing me,
I know you want to be free.
Will it not be good with me?

Will try with all my heart,
I hate it when we are apart.
Need to know where I stand,
Hope you understand.

Don't want me in your life?
Can just let it go,
And live my life without you.
But don't want to.

Just say you want me to be there.
I will say I can be here everyday.

HOW I FEEL

Life can sometimes kick you in the teeth.
When I fall down,
And I get hit hard,
And people disregard.

Don't they care?
And telling me I will go nowhere.
More than unfair,

Why do they want me to cry?
Looking for a reason to try.

Then I think of you,
It's them who don't have a clue.
The love in my heart,
They can not undo.

HOW WILL IT BE?

You're driving me mad, and making me sad.
You know I will always lend you a hand,
Will do anything to make you glad.

When I ask you for a kiss,
Will you take the piss?
If I ask you for a hug,
Will you call me a mug?

I will do anything for your love.
Stop making me feel like a fool, it is not cool.
Stop playing with me, how will it be?

IN THE PARK

Drinking in the park,
Enjoying the dark.
Hate it when we are apart.

As I put my arms around you,
I hope I know what to do.
Can see love in your eyes,
And I will tell you no lies.

Falling into bed,
Will tell you what's in my head.
Want to spend all day with you,
Tomorrow too.

INSIDE

Can't wait to see you again,
I hope you feel the same.
Feels like I'm waiting forever,
Trying to remember.
The good and the bad times,
When you were mine.
Living my life on my own,
Remembering when it was our home.
Know I'll be dreaming of you all night,
Ddon't want to fight.
I remember our last goodbye kiss,
You know this.
It hurts and burns inside,
Will it be better this time?

BLACK HOLE

Wish I could be what you want,
I know I don't mean a lot.
They say go with what you got,
but without you I can not.

Wish I could speak to you again,
only memories remain.
My heart, mind, body and soul,
All lost now inside my mind's black hole.

I don't really feel sad or glad,
And often wonder if I'm going mad.
I'm trying to get on with my life,
But always dream of you being my wife.

LET YOU DOWN

I know I let you down,
That you don't want to see me again.
I wanted love,
What I've got wasn't enough.

Now you hate me,
Never want to see me.
I wish I could explain,
And would do anything to see you again.

Going to live the rest of my life,
This pain hurts like being slashed with a knife.
I wish I could turn back time,
When you were still mine.

Every night when I go to bed,
I try to remember the words you said.
I Need you there,
But know you don't care.

There is nothing I can do,
There is nothing I can say,
I know you don't want me to stay.
Now that your gone I feel like I don't belong.

LIFE

Up high and loving life,
I know you are not my wife.

All my life thinking about what I can and can't see,
with me?
Walking around, with my feet on the ground,
Do you want me around?

Love it when you say,
You want me to stay.
Love to hear you talk,
Love to see you walk.

You know you can with me,
Or tell me to let it be.
Not sure what will be,
But will it be with me?

MISS YOU

I know I have said this before, but I want more.

Can disagree, we can get it for free.

Will it make me cry?

To get there do we need to fly?

Can't we stay here?

You know what I fear.

You told me don't make a sound.

You can look for me, but I won't be found.

MY CAGE

Need to get out of my cell.
All of a sudden my life's turned to hell.
Don't need a push,
Not going to budge an inch.

Then I heard you say, "please stay."
It brightened up my day.
Now that I'm free,
Do you know me?

You changed my life,
I see things in a different way.
Can't believe how it changed,
I'm no longer living in a cage.

MY SOUL

Woke up, thinking this is our home.
You look so good, asked if I could kiss you,
And you said I should.

All my dreams have turned to dust, my soul has rust.
It burns inside, feeling so sad I cried.
Got to find a way to make my self feel better,
But can't pretend. I don't remember.

If only I could talk to you again,
I know you don't feel the same.
Got to continue living my life,
But only enjoyed my time when you were mine.

I've got lots to do,
But keeping busy doesn't stop me from feeling blue.
You know how much I love you,
Is there nothing I can say or do?

NO WAY

You can travel around the world,
Having fun in the sun.
But there is only one place I want to be,
With the one who loves me.

That is now a distant memory,
This is not how it should be.
I really thought we were meant to be,
There is no-one else I want to see.

I can be happy on my own,
I can live my life alone.
But don't want to live the rest of my life,
Knowing you will never be there.

I know you will say you don't care,
And you don't want me there.
It is my fault,
but you won't even give me a chance to explain.
My heart is in so much pain,
Wish I could do it over again.

I want to ask, but I know there is no way.

NOT THERE

Because I was not there,
I know you don't care.
Wish I could change the past,
But I know it's a silly wish.

Can't forgive,
What you did was a sin,.
Don't know, you are not my own.
Do you think you are clever?
What can you remember?

Can you remember why I didn't return?
You just won't learn.
It will forever be that way,
I won't stay,
Not even for a single day.

PEOPLE

They never learn, even when you ask them.
Try to make it as simple as possible,
It is near impossible.
Try to make myself clear, don't want them near.
Time and time again,
Can't communicate with them.
Every time I try, is enough to make me cry.
I will not lie, time does not fly.
Don't know why I try.

TRAITOR OF THE HEART

You are not who I thought you were.
Lied, cheated and hurt my heart.
But still I don't want us to be apart.
I don't know why I feel this way.

You cut me out of your life,
I wanted you to be my wife.

It should not be this way.
You think you can fool them all,
You think hurting people is cool.

PLAYING

Out and about,
Whoring yourself out.

Waiting for the screaming,
When you shout.

Getting high,
No reason to lie.

Waiting for you to cry,
Don't know why I try.

Drink some more,
Only a whore.

When I wake up,
Put on some more make up.

Another day,
Ccoming out to play?

REAL

Do you love me?
When I look into your eyes I can see love.
Am I fooling my self?
Am I living in a dream?
Am I being a fool?
Trying to wake up,
But I'm living the dream.
Spinning sound,
Echoing sound,
Need my feet on the ground.
When I float down.
Will you stay?
Tell me is this for real?

SAID

I already said,
All I have to say.
Do not want me to stay,
Not even for one day.
There is no game I want to play.
Just want to see you today.
And tomorrow will be the same.
Don't know what to say,
Got somewhere else to stay.
When I know what to say.
Please stay.

TART

Walking down the street holding your hand,
Not sure if I understand.

Always in my dreams,
But I'm wide awake.
I will do it for love's sake.
Do I need to give myself a shake?
To make sure I'm awake.

I know I broke your heart,
If only we could go back to the start.
Don't know if I'm being smart,
Or if you're a tart.
But I feel love inside my heart.

THE END

Thinking of days gone by,
Lying in bed remembering the words you said.

Dreaming at night, and when I wake up.
I know I am in love, don't want to give up.

Not like it was years ago,
We both know.
Don't want to let go,
Want you to know.

Need to be a better man,
I'll do what I can.
What I've got is not enough,
But we did fall in love.

Will this feeling ever end?
Has this got to be the end?

TIME AND TIDE

I had the sweetest dream,
Looking deep into your eyes.
Never felt so much love in my life,
Wish you were my wife.

Wish I could spend everyday with you,
I know you will treat me like I don't have a clue.
Want to give you a phone call,
But you will call me a fool.

Didn't we have a good time,
When you were mine?
Time and tide wash everything away,
Even lust turns to dust.

My brains feels scrambled up, had enough.
Everything I do seems pointless without you.

TODAY

I know it's not all about today,
It's fun when we play.
I know when we go out I've got to pay,
Should be that way.

When we are sitting down,
And I look around,
You're the most important person,
In the world.

Hope you know how I feel,
Hope you can trust,
With love and lust.
When that love we had was real.

TOMB

This dreary tomb,
I call my home.
This catacomb,
I call my own.
Where I dwell alone.
With no one calling on the phone,
I am all alone.

I shun all attention,
All human affection.
I want no connection.

The outside world is far away,
It does no matter what they say.
Want no one to stay,
All my love has gone away.
Memories haunt me everyday,
I wish I did it a different way.

Got to get up for another day,
But I know it will be the same.

TOMORROW

I know what they are going to say,
Because it is always the same.
Everyday don't want to play,
The fun in my life has gone away.

They say stuff like ,"chin up and cheer up,"
Or even, "find a new love."
But they don't understand,
None of them can make me glad.

I don't want to feel this sad,
With me was it that bad?
Tomorrow will be another day,
And I will feel the same as today.

WAITING FOR YOU

Will I wait forever?
Are we that clever?
What do you remember?
Even in this cold weather.
All year round,
When you speak I love the sound.
Do you want me around?
Just waiting for you.
I know I never want you to go.

WALKING AROUND

Walking around today,
The words people say.
Always echoing in my head,
What people said.

Is always the same,
They moan and complain.
Then it's time to go to bed again,
Thinking of the girl I love and what she said.

How I feel inside,
I know we cried.
I didn't try heard enough,
And lost my love.

I would do anything,
But now to you,
I don't mean a thing.

A new day will begin,
Was what I did a sin?
Got to get up and walk around again,
Don't want to listen to them.

I know she will never forgive,
Trying to figure out how to live.

WANT IT TO END

You don't own my heart,
You don't even understand art.
Must be something wrong with my head,
Why would I want to take you to bed?
I don't want you to be dead,
Just want you to know what's inside my head.
Need this to end,
Don't even want you as a friend.
Will this feeling ever end?
Want this to end.
Will never be again, don't pretend,
This really is the end.

WANT TO BE ON MY OWN

Want to be alone, everywhere I go.
They never leave me on my own.
Is there nothing I can do,
Don't they have a clue?

Always wanting my attention,
And asking another question.
Will they never learn, want less is the lesson.
Please don't ask another question.

WHO KNOWS?

Can't remember the last time we talked.
Can't remember the last time we walked,
Together.
Trying to remember.
Not trying to be clever,
Will it be never?
Wishing for what is missing.
Not kissing or even close.
Nobody knows.
When it all goes, who knows?

WITHOUT YOU

Miss you like hell,
It's like living in a prison cell.
Living without you,
Has left me not knowing what to do.

Everyday I wake,
Just doing stuff for my own sake.
Wanted to spend my life loving you,
Now I don't have a clue.

So tried and I want to go to bed,
Would you even care if I was dead?
My hearts broken and there is no way to repair,
Don't want anyone else there.

People say talking helps, but won't change a thing.
Emptiness inside won't leave me be.

WON'T RETURN

Crying your eyeballs out.
And more crying, are you lying?
Can't understand what is in your head.
But I listened to every word you said.

Afraid to tell me the truth?
Afraid I would no longer want to share this roof?
Told you I'll leave and never return.
There is no lesson you will learn.

YOUR LOVE

Told you I'd always love you,
And meant what I said.
So many people think words don't matter,
Just stupid chatter.

I know what's important in life,
Wish you were my wife.
All them silly people just come and go,
I don't want to know.

If I ever see you again,
I wouldn't know what to say.
You would just tell me to go away,
and it would not matter what I say.

Not going to lie,
I know you would make me cry.
Is it all my fault?
I feel like a fool.

You won't even let me be a friend,
Will it be that way until the end?
Can't go to my grave knowing you don't care,
Why do I even try?

I'm not good enough to be the one you love.

Published By Broken Hearted Publishing

Printed in Dunstable, United Kingdom